Thomas Jefferson

A Biography of an American President

Table of Contents

Introduction

Thomas Jefferson has a list of achievements as long as an arm. From the beginning, he was destined for greatness because of his ability to learn as well as his skill of being able to produce eloquent writing that could touch both the mind and the soul, bringing people to action. How many Americans can possibly say that they've never heard of Thomas Jefferson or why he's so remembered now?

Much of his fame comes down to the Declaration of Independence that was approved on July 4, 1776. Without that piece of beautiful writing, the course of history for the American people might have been greatly changed. Where would we be now if that document had made its way into the hands of the king of England? However, Jefferson has more than the declaration on his list of achievements. He was a skilled lawyer, a designer, a writer, governor, president, secretary of state, and so much more.

The purpose of this book is to outline and describe the life and times of Thomas Jefferson, one of our most famous founding fathers. Not only will it discuss his prelude to the presidency and his time in office, but it will dig deeper than that. It will focus on his experience with the law, how that led him to the political world, and how his presidency and life afterwards helped create for him a legacy of fighting for freedom. It will also detail his quiet life after the presidency and how he still kept up his pursuit of knowledge even though he had removed himself from public life.

Thomas Jefferson was a man of contradictions, and this, in some ways, was an unfortunate thing. He was a well-born man, highly educated, and yet he enjoyed having small landowners as clients. He spouted freedom as a right and didn't like the idea of control over man and his mind, and yet he owned slaves himself. How can we reconcile with these two opposing things that Jefferson seemed to hold dear?

The point of this book is biographical, and it is not attempting to pardon Jefferson's wrongdoings or false beliefs. It is to focus on what he did do for the country just as it was attempting to break free and begin again from infancy. Thomas Jefferson was there in the thick of it all, right when the Revolution was brewing and after. He had a beautiful dream of democracy that proposed a break from tyranny, freedom, and strengthened the power of the common man. He even said himself:

"I have sworn upon the altar of god, eternal hostility against every form of tyranny over the mind of man."

That was his ultimate goal, to be free in both body and mind, and he wanted that for his beloved new country. Jefferson wrote of freedom, fought for freedom, and believed in the power of that freedom until his dying day. Of course, that would only apply to some people in his mind, but the core of his statements is true and beautiful. It is no surprise, then, that this would be remembered enough to still be taught in schools as well as to be etched for eternity into the side of Mount Rushmore.

Freedom is a wonderful thing, and yet there is more that draws us into learning about Thomas Jefferson and into keeping his name alive to this day. It is his fighting spirit. He was not one to give up on a fight, especially if it was one worth fighting. In some ways, fighting for him was merely the act of continuing despite the difficulty, and learning, gathering knowledge, and improving one's mind and understanding of the world. As is no surprise, Jefferson put it best when he said:

"I hold it that a little rebellion now and then is a good thing, and as necessary in the political world as storms in the physical."

Chapter One: Thomas Jefferson's Childhood and Education

Thomas Jefferson was born on April 13, 1743, to a wealthy, landowning family in Western Virginia. He was born on the slaveholding Shadwell Plantation to Peter Jefferson and Jane Randolph, who were among the wealthiest families in Virginia. Not only that, but his mother was part of the Randolph clan, and she was a part of a line of English and Scottish royalty. Jefferson's father, Peter, was a farmer, a surveyor, and a skilled cartographer. He was known for creating the first accurate map of the Province of Virginia.

He stated that his first childhood memory was that of a fifty-mile journey he took on horseback with a slave of his father's as they traveled to another plantation. Jefferson's father was to manage a friend's estate, and the family traveled there in order to do so. It was there that Jefferson, along with siblings, grew up and began their foray into learning. Jefferson was the third out of ten siblings, and until he was nine, he roamed about the Virginia woods. As a child, his favorite pastimes were playing the violin and reading. He wasn't to begin his schooling until age nine.

Jefferson learned a lot from his father, who was a respected man of business as well as a wealthy planter. Sadly, the man died in 1757, when Jefferson was only 14 and only part of the way through his schooling. But he left behind 7,000 acres of land in Western Virginia, and his family was not left destitute. Jefferson began to look towards his tutors and teachers to guide him in life and direction once his father passed. Unfortunately, we don't know too much about Jane Randolph, although we do know that she passed away in 1776, just as her son had made his true mark in American history.

To Jefferson, knowledge was everything. Because of his upbringing, gaining knowledge became one of his core values, and it showed through his time in school and after. Jefferson began schooling and studying officially when he was nine years old. For most of the year he would stay with a minister who also acted as a teacher, which was not uncommon in those days. He would go to this boarding school until he was sixteen years old, and then, in 1760, he moved on to college, where he attended the College of William and Mary.

Now that his father had passed, Jefferson looked to the knowledgeable peers and professors of his schooling life for guidance and direction. In Jefferson's case, it was a good decision, for their teachings helped steer him toward the path he later found himself on. Once he moved to university, he began studying subjects such as science, rhetoric, mathematics, philosophy, and literature. After two years of studying, he began to study the law under George Wythe who also taught the famous John Marshall and Henry Clay. Jefferson became one of the most highly educated lawyers when he joined the Virginia bar in 1767.

Because of his upbringing and later, his influence in the university, Thomas Jefferson valued education almost more than anything else. He wanted to learn more, be more, and to use his knowledge to analyze and make changes to society if he could.

After university, Jefferson's career as a lawyer began, and he traveled around Virginia, helping to assist with legal matters for those who needed it. It was during this time that he met his future wife, and her name was Martha Wayles Skelton. She was a widow, having lost both her husband and her young child a year before she met Thomas Jefferson. They married on January 1, 1772, and they moved to live at what would later become the famous Monticello.

It was not the beauty it is now when they first moved in, but it was built up and designed over time to become what it is today. What some do not know was that Monticello was built and designed by both Jefferson and his slaves, and most of the furniture inside Monticello was designed by slave labor.

However, before then, he was elected to the House of Burgesses, and he was involved with it from 1769-1774. The political life suited him well, and he seemed to enjoy it, although he didn't prove to be a very good public speaker. However, that didn't dim his enthusiasm or lessen his skill in other important areas.

Chapter Two: Thomas Jefferson's Early Career

When we think of Jefferson now, we don't often think of him as a lawyer. We focus more on his role in writing the important documents that shaped our country and his status as a founding father and president. However, Jefferson was very successful in his work with the law and traveling around allowed him to meet many different types of people and learn more about the American society of which he was a part. Jefferson was able to practice law until 1774 when all the courts were closed because of the impending Revolution.

Jefferson worked in the General Court, and he mostly handled land cases, some of which involved very controversial issues at the time. Most of the cases he dealt with in the beginning were of those who were just trying to make sure that the titles they possessed were real and legitimate. He would do the research within government records to make sure that all was well with the title, and that it in fact did belong to the person in question. This was a very common practice for the time in colonial America.

Jefferson would service various counties throughout Virginia, and at the beginning of his law practice, he was constantly on the move. While it might have been tiring for many others in the same profession, it was a boon for Jefferson as it gave him the chance to see the way of life all across Virginia as well as the burgeoning frontier. He worked with people of various social classes and was able to spot problems in the law and the social system.

He even traveled to gather more clients and to build his own practice. He was often traveling to Williamsburg, and by going there three times a year for many years, he was able to make connections with other lawyers that helped provide him with even more clients.

Jefferson worked with many wealthy landowners to help check if their titles were legitimate as well as assist them in legal matters pertaining to their land, but mostly, he represented smaller landowners, and he seemed to prefer it that way. Jefferson was greatly in support of small, hardworking landowners. But he was concerned, as were many others, by what he was beginning to see in the backcountry of Virginia and elsewhere.

Just like in England, there were a few select families who owned the majority of the land. It was very much like the nobility in England, and he was afraid that eventually, America would just simply be a copy of England in the way it handled its land laws.

Not only did he help various families with this issue during his time as a lawyer, but later, we can see how this experience affected his ideas about how land should be managed when fighting for independence from England. He helped to write laws that would remove the old land laws taken from England; that the eldest son of a family would inherit all and that the land could only remain in the possession of one male heir. The ideas for a new sort of country separate from England and her rules were beginning to grow.

Jefferson's First Writing and the Path to Revolution

Once the Revolution began to build, so did anti-British sentiments. The American colonies had built themselves up for so many years and were feeling their strength. Because of the French and Indian War in 1763, Britain was left with some major financial issues. Therefore, they looked to their various colonies to help support them using the age-old tactic of taxation. First, there was the Stamp Act in 1765, putting a tax on printed goods. That made the colonists' absolutely furious, and that was the impetus for the creation of the famous words "no taxation without representation."

Then, of course, in 1773, came the infamous Boston Tea Party, a reaction to the tyrannical tea tax that the king imposed on the colonies. Rebellion was on the minds of the people, and things began to heat up and head towards revolution as a solution. In 1775, the first battles of the Revolution began, which were the Battles of Lexington and Concord.

Jefferson joined in the fight from the beginning, and he showed his support for the American cause by writing, "A Summary of the Rights of British America" written in 1774.

In this essay, he focused on:

- Natural rights

- The disagreement with the Parliament's control over the colonies any longer

- The lack of connection with the things of Britain except for the king

The main focus of his arguments was that he didn't believe Britain's Parliament had any right to govern them or to create laws that restricted them. They had been working well enough for many years without England's influence, and once that was being threatened, everything changed. It was this powerful essay that helped push Thomas Jefferson into the foreground. Before, he was just a country lawyer, but now, he was fighting for American independence using his knowledge and his skill of writing. Now, he became known as a symbol, along with other famed patriots such as Patrick Henry, who would do whatever they could to fight for their country against the tyranny of Britain.

In 1774, after the publication of this first public writing, he retired from working as a lawyer and turned over his practice to someone else. Jefferson became a part of the Continental Congress and was a member from 1775-1776. Within that group, he was chosen along with Ben Franklin, John Adams, Robert Livingstone, and Roger Sherman to create the Declaration of Independence. While the battles began and the war was brewing, he, however, was the mastermind behind the famed document and wrote it all on his own, while some of the others edited it and gave him their opinions and input. He was selected for the job for his ability to write in an eloquent yet penetrating fashion.

This was what Thomas Jefferson was most famous for, and it was most definitely something to be envious of; his skill with the written word, and the beauty and genius that was the Declaration of Independence. Once the work was complete, Jefferson presented it to the Continental Congress. After some debate about certain content in reference to King George III, the group revised it and finalized the piece to be sent to the king in England.

Most do not know that the Continental Congress never called the declaration as we know it by its title today. Its original title was "The Unanimous Declaration of the 13 United States of America". The declaration was approved on July 4.

After he wrote the declaration, it was sent to King George III to read, and a nation waited for what would happen next. Feelings of freedom and breaking away from the old life were brewing. Hope and fear were mixed with anticipation. Thomas Jefferson was right there in the middle of it all, using his knowledge and ability to assist in gaining independence for the country he so loved.

His work would help to create a beautiful foundation for the nation, and his writing showed just what kind of country he wanted America to be: free, egalitarian, and representative.

Chapter Three: Jefferson's Other Political Ventures Pre-Presidency

In our minds, we often group Jefferson's achievements together, as if they happened right after the other. His writing of the declaration with the Revolution as a backdrop and his presidency is foremost in people's minds when they think of the famed political leader. However, he had plenty of other experience with politics before he delved into life in the White House to lead the nation. As mentioned previously, for a long while he worked as a lawyer, dealing with land issues, traveling around Virginia to help clients and to build his law practice. Then, after the Continental Congress and the sending off of the Declaration, he entered into other aspects of political life.

Virginia House of Delegates

Jefferson had already served in the Virginia House of Burgesses for a few years, and during that time, he worked to create the Virginia Committee of Correspondence. This was one of the committees filled with political rebels who wished to weaken the tyrannical hold on the colonies that Britain had.

But after the declaration, Jefferson got himself elected in 1776 to the Virginia House of Delegates, in which he served until 1779. It was during this time that he worked to abolish those terrible land laws that America had brought over from England: entail and primogeniture. Entail is the rule that land must only be in possession by one male heir, and the land must be held accountable for debts taken on by those in the family. Primogeniture was the rule that land must pass to the eldest son, forsaking any other family members.

It was also during this time in the House of Delegates that Jefferson wrote another piece, called "Virginia Bill for Establishing Religious Freedom." The purpose of this document was to help break the connection between religion and the government which was so prevalent at the time in Europe. Jefferson, with his own religious beliefs, didn't think that religion had any real place in government issues, actions, or practices.

Jefferson believed that when religion got involved with other areas of life, it was a hindrance or a barrier to gaining knowledge and becoming the best that one could possibly be. He didn't view God as a being with whom to have a relationship, but rather the creator of the world, who left it in the hands of humans to do with it what they could.

Jefferson believed in the power of the mind and that it could bring about a better society once they were freed from British oppression and tyranny. He was a huge advocate of free education, and he fought for that while in the House of Delegates. But of course, the free education was only for white, male Virginia residents at the time. He wanted freedom and empowerment of man, and that's what we remember him for, but it's also important to remember that he was a man of his time. He wanted freedom and liberation and education for *men* who were *white,* and that's it.

Governor of Virginia

After his time serving in the House of Delegates, Jefferson was elected Governor of Virginia in 1779, and he held this position until 1781. Unfortunately, during his two-year stint, he didn't get the power over decision-making that might have been expected. He had no veto power, and there was an eight-man council that was above him.

Therefore, he wasn't able to push forward the legislation he wanted during this time. As the Revolutionary War raged on, and British soldiers began to flock to the colonies to beat their colonists into submission, they took over Richmond, VA. Jefferson was forced to leave his home and find a place of safety for his family. But this choice didn't seem to match his previous statements or actions relating to revolution and fighting for freedom against tyranny. Many saw this as a coward's actions, and it worked to slightly tarnish his reputation.

The Aftermath

Jefferson saw this as a terrible blow as well as a sort of failure, and he eventually left that position and sort of hid away for a little while, returning home. His wife, Martha, was gravely ill, and sadly, she died on November 6, 1782, in childbirth with her sixth child. Despite whispers of affairs, Jefferson loved his wife dearly, and he was heartbroken by her death. He spent the next little while focusing his attention at home, and he even authored his very first and only book, *Notes on the State of Virginia*.

In this book, it reiterated all the statements he'd made in the past about freedoms, education, and the abolishment of British land laws that kept land in the hands of the elite. He wanted land to be widely distributed, and he wanted a different system than was present before under English rule. He also:

- Expressed his fears about what would happen post-Revolution

- Stated that he opposed slavery

- Yet believed that black people were inferior in all ways to whites and would not have the same capabilities

This book was written during his time away from public life between 1781 and 1783. It was later published in 1785. This book is interesting because it outlines what Jefferson truly thought about the state of the nation, the war, and slavery, all hot issues at the time. For example, even though he ran away from the English when they arrived in Virginia, he still believed in the essence of the revolution. And even though he believed in freedom, land distribution, and free education, he still held true to the beliefs he had about those of other races.

Despite whatever feelings he might have had about the non-white races, there is some DNA evidence to suggest that he had at least one affair with one of his slaves. Her name was Sally Hemings, and she was actually Mrs. Jefferson's half-sister, having been fathered by Mrs. Jefferson's father and then later given to Jefferson upon his marriage to Martha. Some evidence shows that Jefferson might have been the father of all of Sally's children, which numbered six at the end.

He had slaves for his whole life, and his success with Monticello and the land he owned was due to slave labor. But in many of his writings, he did state that he believed slavery should be abolished. However, he didn't think that freed slaves should stay in the states, but that they should be returned to their home continent of Africa.

Return to Political Life

Despite his earlier plans to stay at Monticello and live out the life of a country gentleman for the rest of his days, he returned to political life in 1783. The states were still in the midst of war with Britain at this time, but it was soon nearing to a close. He was appointed to the Confederation Congress as the representative for Virginia, and he agreed to take on the role. This Congress took place in Philadelphia, and so he spent much of his time there.

During his time as part of the Confederation Congress, he took part in many important acts. But later that year, the Treaty of Paris was signed. It officially ended the Revolutionary War on September 3, 1783. But even the year prior, the colonies and Britain had started peace talks. Jefferson was appointed to join in these talks and travel to Britain to do so, but he had travel delays, and so he missed out.

Now that the war was finally over after so many long years, the newly freed United States had to make plans to stand on its own two feet. Also in 1784, Jefferson, still part of the Confederation Congress, helped to write a document that established some government control for the Western territories.

Once the territories reached a certain population level, they could lobby for statehood.

Minister to France

Benjamin Franklin was originally the minister to France, but Jefferson replaced him in 1785. It was an old way of saying ambassador, and they would perform similar duties. Jefferson had great success in the role, and he enjoyed his time in France. He worked as minister to France from 1785 to 1789. But what's particularly interesting is, he got to be there during the time of France's own revolution.

He was able to see the vast differences between the elite and the poor classes, and he hated it, just as he had when he saw similar class systems showing up in the US when they were still under British rule. He enjoyed the luxury of France, but he didn't like the government situation, and the French Revolution only heightened their problems. He returned to the United States after five years there, and he came back home, happy to return to what he believed was the true and right way for a country to govern itself.

Secretary of State

It must have been quite satisfying to return to his own country, still in its infancy as a self-governing nation, and see its success while the country he was just in was still struggling to survive from the chaos and violence of its revolution. Jefferson's next political venture came in the form of becoming a cabinet member. In the same year that he returned to the US, the country's very first president was unanimously elected to office. George Washington became president, and he was thrilled at Jefferson's return, telling him that he'd selected him to be the first secretary of state.

Initially, Jefferson wasn't very excited to take up this position. Understandably, it could possibly have been because he had moved from one intense life and career move to another. He helped a country get through its revolution, having written documents that changed a nation. Then he became governor; his wife died; he worked with the Confederation Congress, and then he moved on to work as minister to France. It wouldn't be surprising if he wasn't interested in the cabinet member position because he was flat out exhausted from all the political work he'd been getting into.

However, he was less excited about the position because of one of the other cabinet members that had been chosen: Alexander Hamilton. This younger man became the Secretary of the Treasury, and he was considered one of Washington's most trusted advisors. While Washington favored Jefferson greatly, and that's why he chose him, it seemed more and more as time went on that he was being more affected by Hamilton's influence.

Hamilton, despite the fact that the Revolutionary War was over, and they were free from Britain's clutches, wanted to use England as a model in many ways, especially economically. Jefferson fiercely disagreed and wished to look more to France for inspiration and connection. Jefferson, as could be expected, was heavily anti-British and wanted a completely separate sort and style of government.

Hamilton supported a strong centralized Federal government, which Jefferson also opposed. He also wanted to take a position of neutrality when it came to foreign (European) issues, and he liked the idea of a general, broad understanding of the Constitution. On the other hand, Jefferson wanted states to have power over their own people; he wanted to read the Constitution with a strict, literal understanding, and he was hoping to be the recipient of some support from France now that their revolution was over.

Washington had a bit of an interesting situation on his hands, seeing that two of his advisors were polar opposites in their political views. This was the birth of a divergence in the US political world and the creation of two political parties.

Hamilton was the representative of the party called the Federalists, and Jefferson led the party called the Republicans or Democratic-Republicans as it was called then. He served as the secretary of state from 1790 to 1793, and he later resigned from the position and returned to Monticello to decompress after so much action.

It was time for him to relax and spend time at his home and with his family for a little while before he would return to politics.

Chapter Four: From Vice-President to President

Jefferson took time off after his three-year stint as secretary of state, and he rested in Monticello. It was during these three years that he made considerable changes and improvements to his home.

While he might have thought that his time in the spotlight was over, it was anything but. Three years after he left office as secretary of state, he was called back in 1796. His political party, the Republicans, had put him forth as a candidate for the next presidential election. George Washington had served his two terms of four years, and now it was time for someone else to take the reins.

The man who ran opposite him was John Adams, the former vice-president of George Washington, and he was a Federalist. Jefferson waited to hear the vote (instead of campaigning, which wasn't done for elections until later), and he lost to Adams. Instead, he became the vice-president. Sadly, the former friendship between Adams and Jefferson was not what it once was because of their very opposite political views. During office, they didn't convene or discuss issues with one another as might have been hoped for or expected in that kind of position.

Because of this, Jefferson had more time on his hands than might have been originally expected. He used it to write "A Manual of Parliamentary Practice", and it was used as a guide for Congress for many years after it was originally written. He also helped to fan into flame the Republican's anger towards the Federalist party. Opposition was brewing and growing, and it would help change things for the next presidential election in 1800, where tensions were high, and the first real competition for president occurred.

The Election of 1800: Jefferson vs. Adams and Burr

By the time 1800 rolled around, the difficulties between the Democratic-Republicans had come to a head as well as the deep differences between those within the Federalist parties. Many of the Federalist members (think Hamilton) had much more extreme Federalist views about how they wanted the country to run. But Adams was more on the moderate side, so when it came time for him to run again, he found himself not supported by many members of his party.

The Republicans desperately wanted Jefferson as their candidate for the presidency because he was the embodiment of their main ideals: states' rights, assisting France, less centralized government, etc. This time, a little more wisely, they took another member from their party, Aaron Burr, hoping to make him the vice-president. But because of a flaw in the voting system, Burr and Jefferson ended up in a tie!

This tie took some time to resolve, and it was sent to the House of Representatives to deal with. Eventually, it was settled, and Thomas Jefferson became the United States' third president to take office, and Aaron Burr became his vice-president. When he became president and gave his inaugural address, he was hoping to unite the nation again. It had become so broken through the fighting between parties and within parties.

However, his party was currently standing strong because they had come together during the divisiveness of the Federalists. Not only that, but this was a huge event worldwide because the power had transferred from one party (the Federalists) to another (the Democratic-Republicans), and there was no violence involved.

In his inaugural address, he tried to remind people of what brought them together and the fact that they truly were fighting for the same things. Jefferson said "We have called by different names brethren of the same principle. We are all Republicans; we are all Federalists."

Perhaps it was an attempt to placate, or it really was a hope and an attempt to unite a nation, to keep them from fracturing based on party differences as had so many other nations before it. The world was watching closely as America made this peaceful transition, and Jefferson knew it. He was likely hoping to continue as they had done and to make better what they were currently struggling with.

Federalists Fighting Back!

While it was a peaceful transition, the Federalists still wanted to find a way to retain some of their power while Jefferson was in office. At first, during his election time, they hoped to spread the word that he was just a godless man, seeking to destroy the ideals of the country. It was the first time such heated competition between parties was so obvious. As mentioned before, there was a tie between Jefferson and Burr because Adams had lost all his popularity.

The Federalists were at a loss, and Hamilton, a Federalist of the most extreme, hated Burr and convinced many other Federalists to send in a blank ballot as a solution. This helped to give Jefferson the victory, and Burr was furious when he found out what Hamilton had done. In the future, Burr and Hamilton were to have a duel in which he killed Hamilton after shooting him through the chest.

Jefferson was now selected as the next president, but there was still a chance to keep some Federalists in power. Lucky for them, by 1800, all of the Supreme Court justices were Federalists because Congress had been a Federalist majority under both Washington and Adams. Before Jefferson took office, this Congress put out the Judiciary Act of 1801, and this limited the justices to five instead of six. It also included a new circuit system with a lot of new clerks, judges, and other staff, who were all Federalists of course. Adams signed all their commissions before he left office, hoping they'd be appointed as soon as possible once Jefferson took his place.

However, James Madison, who took over as secretary of state when Jefferson became president, helped to prevent some of these commissions from ever getting sent. And under Jefferson's rule, new Republican members of the Congress helped to repeal the Judiciary Act which helped to stop those hurried commissions which slipped through the cracks. But the Supreme Court justices couldn't be changed. Just like today, they retain this position for life.

Therefore, some of Jefferson's decisions and acts were hindered by this. The Federalists were willing to do anything to get in the way of having a Democratic-Republican come in and "destroy" the nation and the work they'd done thus far. But they might have been pleasantly surprised or maybe impressed by all that Jefferson was about to accomplish.

The First Term

As president, once the tension had passed about a Republican taking office away from a Federalist, Jefferson got to work on his duties. He is considered one of America's greatest and most successful presidents because of all he did. He was successful, especially in his first few years because he worked on something that is still an issue of contention today: tax reduction.

Jefferson focused a lot on fixing the economic issues in the states. His accomplishments to this end are as follows:

- He cut the US budget
- He greatly reduced the spending of the Navy as well as the army
- He got rid of the whiskey tax
- He cut down the national debt by about 33%
- He sent a naval force to deal with pirates in the Mediterranean who were causing issues for US ships
- He made the Louisiana Purchase in 1803

All of these accomplishments were in his first term as president. He was quick, efficient, and he got things done. It was no wonder, then, that he won "by a landslide", as they say, in the next election in 1804.

The Louisiana Purchase

This is one of the most famous things that Jefferson did during his presidency. Most high school students would know the basic background of this story and Jefferson's involvement. Jefferson made this choice at the end of his first term in 1803, however, it began earlier than that. In 1800, Spain had quietly sold some of the lands they held in North America to France. When Jefferson found out about it, he sent some ministers to France to try and negotiate a deal.

Robert Livingston and James Monroe were the ministers sent to France to make land negotiations with Napoleon. Now, this would have been a tricky situation. France had finished its revolution as well as the crazed aftermath. But while Jefferson was partial to France and her problems, he didn't have an interest in having France remain side by side with the newly formed union. So, he wanted to make them a deal, and Napoleon was interested in selling his land.

Napoleon was happy to sell because he was interested in getting money to fund a new war with England. Jefferson had some qualms about this, but he agreed, and Napoleon offered to sell it to the US for $15 million for 828,000 square miles, which came out to about 4 cents per acre. It was an amazing deal, and Jefferson took it. He did have some hesitation about this as well because the Constitution didn't mention anything about what to do in the case of purchasing foreign lands. Jefferson was a strict reader of the Constitution, so he thought this should be amended later.

Despite his misgivings, he made the purchase, and it was approved five months later by Congress. This choice helped to double the land of the United States. Because they needed to "check on their investment", Jefferson sent a party of explorers to go and see what lay in the land beyond. He sent Meriweather Lewis and William Clark out to explore the new addition to the states, along with twenty-five other men.

This was a turning point for the US in more ways than one. Jefferson put some distance between himself and Napoleon who would go on to start a war just as he'd planned. Jefferson also expanded his nation which would bring with it more resources, more opportunities, and simply more land. More land is more power, and it helped to build the young nation and move it on from its stage of infancy. He left his first term as a hero.

Jefferson's Second Term

At this stage, Jefferson seemed unstoppable. He slid into office for another term of four years, and he was very popular and well-liked among those in his party. They believed him to be the savior of the nation, and he had accomplished so much in such a short amount of time. But all good things can come to an end, of course, as we've seen in many, many other presidencies. Or rather, everyone can make mistakes.

During this time, the Napoleonic Wars were in full swing. They began in 1803 and lasted for many years. Initially, America got involved by supplying materials to each power, and both Britain and France attempted to stop the others' access to that aid. America was doing fabulously economically and earning a lot of money through exportation and merchant supplies.

However, because Britain and France were trying to undermine each other, they each did their best to try and stop American ships from getting to their enemy. Both Britain and France worked hard to harass those American ships which did make it through.

Jefferson, seeing the problem, decided to cut ties once and for all. He created the Embargo Act of 1807. This outlawed all shipping with Europe, and it hugely decreased the recent income the US was making through all their exports. Things went downhill from there, and exports went down from $108 million to $22 million, and many US citizens were furious with their president for having made that choice

Jefferson had hopes that it would make the warring countries respect the US and its power, but it didn't really pan out as he'd hoped. He later changed the act, to ban trade only with England and France, but the rest of Europe was open for trading to the US. But it was too late, and he was soon to end his second term as president, anyway.

No doubt, businessmen of all kinds were in an uproar about the Embargo Act, and likely, the economy kept going down after Jefferson left office in 1809 as a result. Despite his efforts to fix what he'd done, he didn't realize that this economically disastrous decision would bring America into another war a few years later, again with their former mother country: the War of 1812.

Chapter Five: Life Beyond the White House

As happened previously, following his stint as Governor of Virginia, it was time for Jefferson to return to Monticello. This time it would be for the rest of his days. After he left office in 1809, he once more sought safe haven in his now beautiful and impressive home. His former secretary of state and good friend, James Madison, took his place as the fourth president of the US. Jefferson was to live another 17 years, and during this time, he became known as "The Sage of Monticello".

Jefferson was more suited to the solitary life. He had taken a massive role in the political goings-on of the United States, but he enjoyed his solitude. As mentioned earlier, Jefferson was not a very good speaker, and so he preferred to stay away from public speaking situations. He did, however, enjoy having guests visit him, and sometimes, there might have been as many as fifty guests dining and visiting Monticello in a night.

Upon his return to Monticello, Jefferson continued a routine of study, horseback riding while he was still feeling well, and of course, letter-writing.

Correspondence

This was a time of letter writing in Jefferson's life. He had much more time than he had before, and he spent it in constant communication between himself and friends, relatives, and political acquaintances. Some of these people were also not located in the country, as he had a vast group of acquaintances and friends from all over the world.

Some of the people he corresponded with regularly were former friends and political rival John Adams, as well as Dr. Benjamin Rush, James Madison, and John Tyler. Earlier in his life, when John Adams and he were good friends, Jefferson and Adams' wife, Abigail became very dear friends, and they corresponded regularly for a long while. But because of the situation with the political tension between the two men, Abigail was torn, and she had to support her husband. She might even have tried to speak to Adams about reconciliation once the years had passed. But in the end, it was Adams who broke the ice in 1812 when he wrote a letter to Jefferson, the first contact they'd had in a long time.

What was so touching about his correspondence with John Adams is that they seemed to make up for the past and come to a sort of reconciliation in their old age. In response to Adams, Jefferson wrote:

"A letter from you calls up recollections very dear to my mind. It carries me back to the times when, beset with difficulties and dangers, we were fellow laborers in the same cause, struggling for what is most valuable to man, his right of self-government. Laboring always at the same oar, with some wave ever ahead threatening to overwhelm us and yet passing harmless under our bark, we knew not how, we rode through the storm with heart and hand, and made a happy port."

Leave it to Thomas Jefferson to write only the best letter of reconciliation with very carefully chosen words. Similar to his inaugural speech before his first term, Jefferson wanted unity. He wanted to believe that everyone shared those same principles, even if on the surface, they disagreed about a few things. It was true; he and John Adams were there right from the start, and together, they helped to build a new nation. At the end of the letter, Jefferson signed off with:

"I feel in these particulars respecting yourself; none have suspended for one moment my sincere esteem for you; and I now salute you with unchanged affections and respect."

In Monticello, Jefferson left behind the world of politics and focused on improving his relationships as well as his mind, and his correspondence is evidence of that.

Jefferson and Study

Just like he had before, Jefferson dedicated himself to his studies. He read, designed, and experimented. Jefferson focused on natural history, science, and he also worked on inventions as well as research. This was the time when he really dedicated himself to spending a lot of money on continuing to build up his beautiful house. However, it cost him a great deal of money to do so and that would come to hurt him in the end.

Jefferson and the American Philosophical Society

Jefferson even continued as president of the American Philosophical Society until 1815. This society is the oldest academic or learning-focused society in the United States. It was founded in 1743 by none other than Benjamin Franklin, and despite a brief hiatus, the society continued. Jefferson was elected to be part of it in 1780.

Jefferson's part in this society affected other events that happened during his political life. He served on something called the "Bone Committee", a committee created to finding and collecting various skeletal remains of the wooly mammoth. He even included William Clark in his actions to further this committee's cause in 1807. He asked the man to lead a dig that happened at Big Bone Lick, KY, and Clark sent Jefferson over

300 bones that they'd found there. Jefferson sent many to the American Philosophical Society that they didn't already have among their bone collection.

When he sent Lewis and Clark out on the expedition to explore the west, he used contacts within the society to assist them in their information and research. The society also received the information that Lewis and Clark were able to send back from their time out there. In 1797, they elected Jefferson as president of the society, and he kept that position until 1815. He tried to resign on several occasions, but they didn't allow it. Even when he moved away back to Monticello in 1809, he kept up to date with the meetings because they sent him information on the minutes.

By the end, he was growing old and a bit sickly, so they had to accept his final resignation. But even after he died, they had so much respect for him, that they covered his president's chair in black for six months. This society was something that Jefferson remained a part of through the most tumultuous times of his life: vice-presidency and then the presidency. Amazingly, he was able to keep up with so much despite everything else that was going on in his political life. That goes to show just how much he respected knowledge, valued continued learning, and appreciated fellow like-minds.

The University of Virginia

Probably Jefferson's greatest "contribution" or "result" of his long and final stint at Monticello was the University of Virginia. This was something he was incredibly passionate about, and he made this clear by how much he spent time creating it. He designed the campus, and it was the very first secular university in the United States, which was a crowning achievement in his mind.

Jefferson wanted everything to be perfect, and he worked hard to create the greatest university for the people of his home state. He wanted a place where people could come to focus on and advance their knowledge. Again, his passion for knowledge and advancement in learning is seen in his final act on earth: to bring people together to learn and study.

Jefferson was the one who was the "jack of all trades" to the university. He designed the buildings, built the curriculum, chose the teachers, and was happy to be a part of it. It was founded in 1819, but luckily, Jefferson was still alive when the university opened up, ready for enrollment on March 7, 1825.

It must have been an incredible relief and delight to watch as the long-awaited work of his hands had come to life. It was perhaps very similar to the way he felt watching his home take shape under his direction. He likely felt that these were the incredible contributions he was leaving behind him. Beauty, knowledge, and advancement above all things.

Financial Troubles

Despite all the wonderful things that Jefferson was bringing to the world and hoping to leave behind, he did leave something else behind and that was financial troubles. It's interesting that that would have happened to him after he spent much of his presidency attempting to help cut the national debt and keep the United States out of harm's way, economically and in many other ways.

But due to the cost of building and making improvements to his house as well as hosting guests and working on the university, Jefferson was in great debt towards the end of his life. He needed some way to pay off the debts that were growing rather substantially, especially when he became so ill that he needed medicine and a doctor's attention. He sold much of his library to the United States government.

During the War of 1812, a lot of the White House had been burned, and so much of its library was lost. So, Jefferson saw the opportunity to pay off his debts, and (again) spread and promote knowledge, and because of his contribution, it was the start of the Library of Congress.

By the end of his life, he still had many slaves on his property. At the height of his slave ownership, he had about 150, and that number was not too far off by the end of his days, although he had to use many of them as collateral because of his debts. He might have considered freeing them, but he needed them to pay back his creditors once he was passed. And he also stated that he didn't want to free them because he, as mentioned in a previous chapter, didn't believe they would do well to live as freemen alongside men who were formerly their masters.

Family

Jefferson had lived a long time as a widow, for his wife died in 1782 after a difficult childbirth. She had struggled with each new birth, and after the last one, her body was spent. With his wife Martha, Jefferson became the father of six children. But as was not surprising for the time, only two of them lived to make it to adulthood. These were two women named Martha and Mary, which the family called Patsy and Polly.

He was heartbroken at the loss of his wife, and his daughter stated that she remembered him locking himself away in his room after her death. Even though he had a long-standing affair with one of his slaves, Sally Hemings, with whom he had many children according to common belief, he had been devoted to his wife.

Sadly, one daughter married and died in 1804, and she had only one surviving child. It was Martha who was able to be there with her father at the end. At the end of his life, his final child, many grandchildren, and great-grandchildren became a focus of his life. He was visited by them often, and they were there to surround him at his deathbed.

Chapter Six: The Death of Thomas Jefferson and His Legacy

Thomas Jefferson had lived a long and very eventful life. He had seen many things in his time, experienced many triumphs, and felt many sorrows. Jefferson had been a very privileged man, having grown up in a good, wealthy family with access to education and resources that other men didn't have. It helped to allow him to develop his intellect and showcase it to the world. We can only wonder what Thomas Jefferson was feeling at the end of his days as he felt his health slipping with the knowledge that he would not be long for this world.

Did he think often of his achievements? Or did he focus more on his failings and disappointments, his griefs and sorrows? We'll never know.

The End of His Days

At the end of his life, he became less mobile. He was suffering from rheumatic pain as well as an enlarged prostate. His real cause of death isn't totally clear, but we can make a few guesses because he mentioned his struggle with certain symptoms in various letters. He had been struggling with rheumatism since

1818, and he visited Warm Springs, VA to find himself some relief through soaking in mineral baths.

Mysteriously, he got an infection on his buttcheek which took the shape of a nasty boil. This affected him greatly, and while the doctor was able to clear it up, the use of mercury might have been the cause of future bowel issues such as diarrhea. Once the boil was cleared, Jefferson still continued his riding and former tasks. He would also keep to his writing and his studies.

By the mid-1820s, Jefferson was suffering from these bowel symptoms along with many other strange, perhaps-related things such as partial deafness, weak joints, swollen legs, a boil on his jaw, and a lowered immune system, causing him to often fall ill. He did his best to keep up with his usual routine when he was feeling up to it, but he must have known that his time was soon near. When these symptoms started getting worse, Jefferson was around 80 years old.

Then, in 1825, about a year before his death, Jefferson continued to have diarrhea, but he also wrote to James Monroe, telling him that he was unable to urinate without pain. The doctor who was the doctor there at the end of his life, Dr. Robley Dunglison, discovered that the issue was an enlarged prostate. He was able to use a tool made of elastic gum which would be inserted through the urethra to help create room for the urine to flow.

This provided great relief, of course, but it added other problems to Jefferson's already growing list of ailments. Germ theory was not yet around, so according to what we know, it's likely that Jefferson also started to suffer from a kidney infection on top of his prostate issues. He was bedridden at this time, but he would still try to write as best he could. This was a man willing to fight to the end to retain his greatest attribute: his sharp and well-formed mind.

Sadly, due to all the illnesses wracking the old man's body, he was basically in a sort of daze during the days before his death in 1826, and would only awaken at certain times. It was July, and the time was nearing to celebrate the 50th anniversary of the Declaration of Independence. He, along with Adams, who was also very ill and on the brink of death, was invited to the White House. There was to be a great celebration for the Fourth of July. Unfortunately, he couldn't attend due to his immobility and pain.

He died on July 4, 1826, and the story goes that his doctor whispered in his ear just before his death that he'd made it to the Fourth of July. Jefferson was buried in the family plot at Monticello, finally joining his wife once more in death. He wrote his tombstone's inscription as well, and it can tell us something about him and what he thought of himself at the end of his life. His inscription states:

"Here was buried Thomas Jefferson, author of the Declaration of American Independence and of the Virginia Statute for Religious Freedom, and father of the University of Virginia."

He didn't write about his political achievements in terms of making changes to the country or building it up. The inscription is more factual rather than about tooting his own horn. Oddly, it didn't even mention his time as president. And he was buried at his home in Virginia and not in a public cemetery in DC. This is a man who achieved much and yet still showed his humility as well as his focus on the ideas he contributed rather than the positions he held.

Coincidentally, John Adams also died on the Fourth just a few hours later in Massachusetts.

Family Drama

Even though many of Jefferson's accomplishments in his vast life seem almost superhuman, the family drama he experienced towards the end of his life made him very much human. While his family life was generally free of trouble, and there was a lot of love between him, his daughters, and his grandchildren, there was some trouble that brewed between his two sons-in-law. These were the husbands of Martha and Mary.

Martha's husband was named Thomas Mann Randolph, and Mary's husband was named John Wayles Eppes.

There was even some trouble between Thomas Mann Randolph and his oldest son Thomas Jefferson Randolph, whose nickname was Jeff. This trouble gave a lot of stress and problems to Jefferson's beloved daughter Martha, and it caused a rift between her and her husband until Thomas Mann Randolph was close to death in 1828. They were able to come to some kind of reconciliation at that point.

But the trouble didn't end there. Unfortunately, Thomas Jefferson's oldest granddaughter, Ann Cary Randolph Bankhead married an alcoholic named Charles Lewis Bankhead, and this man often physically fought with Thomas Jefferson Randolph, Jefferson's other grandson. On one particular occasion, in 1819, Jefferson had to ride to assist his wounded grandson, even though Jefferson was struggling with his own health at the time.

In addition, Jefferson wasn't the only one with pecuniary issues. One of his sons-in-law also had financial troubles, and the family looked to Jefferson to assist them. Or Jefferson took it upon himself to help even though he was struggling to support himself and the land he owned as well as the people he had working under him. He also had to help support the education as well as the marriages of many of his grandchildren. In the end, he was beset with troubles from all sides and of all kinds, but the family who loved him was there for him. He died surrounded by those he loved and for whom he had given himself.

Jefferson's Legacy and Impact

The number of things that Jefferson was able to accomplish in a lifetime is a bit humbling. In today's world, we have so much to distract us and keep us from expanding our minds or working towards our goals. Jefferson had the gift of time and money, even though he was struggling with major debts at the end of his life. Jefferson lived to the age of 83, and he was only completely bedridden and unable to function in the last few days of his life.

He had more time than most people were given in that period, and he used it to the greatest advantage. Until the end, he believed in the rights of self-government and religious freedoms. He thought that the mind of man could accomplish anything with the right tools and materials. He didn't think they should depend upon God to serve them when they could serve themselves by using knowledge to guide them.

He was the father of the Declaration of Independence, and those words still ring in American hearts today. Even though he was a man full of contradictions, the actual words that he wrote down about equality and freedom are what America can aspire to be and strive for. Even after hundreds of years, we're still not getting everything right. We are a flawed nation, but Jefferson helped to establish in many ways what America *should* be.

Ultimately, Jefferson's major accomplishments included:

- Writing the "A Summary of the Rights of British America"
- Writing the Declaration of Independence
- Serving in the House of Delegates and Burgesses
- Acting as Governor of Virginia
- Writing his book Notes on the State of Virginia
- Acting as Minister to France
- Working as secretary of state to George Washington
- Serving as vice president under John Adams
- Serving as president of the USA for two terms
- President of the American Philosophical Society
- Designer and founder of the University of Virginia
- Father, statesman, friend, student, teacher, and sage

Throughout it all, and no matter what struggles he went through, he still maintained his beliefs and his position. As he wrote to John Adams at the end of his life, they were both working at the "same oar," and he stayed strong in his ideals until his dying day. What he'd achieved during his life and the way he stayed firm is partly what has made him so popular and given him such a legacy as he has.

Chapter Seven: Things You Might Not Have Known About America's Third President

In history, there are always things skipped or glossed over. In school, we're often taught the main points, but there isn't always time to get down into the nitty-gritty. Sometimes, that's where the most interesting things are revealed! Just like any other president, there are a few things about Thomas Jefferson that are not as widely known, and they add a little bit more color to the portrait of the famous man.

1) Jefferson loved wine!

Jefferson was something of a wine connoisseur. While living in France, he learned even more, and he brought back his knowledge and passion for French wine when he returned to the States. He was one of the great wine connoisseurs at this point in America. He even had two vineyards created at Monticello! His love of wine and the consumption of it were partly to blame for his financial troubles towards the end of his life.

2) Books were everything to him.

Jefferson is known to have said that he couldn't survive without books. Books were his gateway to the knowledge and skill that he used to create everything around him. Without them, he would not have been the man he turned out to be. When he donated some of his library to the US government, which started the Library of Congress, he donated about 6,500 books.

He encouraged the pursuit of reading in his family. He loved children, and when his grandchildren came to visit him, he enjoyed their visits thoroughly and taught them many fun games. However, he did try to instill a love and a habit of reading. One of his grandchildren named Virginia Jefferson Randolph Trist recalled a memory that in the evening, they would all follow the example of their grandfather and take up a book to read. Occasionally, she would catch him looking up at them all as they read and smiling.

3) Jefferson was fascinated by archaeology and paleontology.

As mentioned in a previous chapter, Jefferson had a great interest in archaeology and uncovering prehistoric animals. The prehistoric animal he was most interested in was the mammoth. During his tenure as the president of the American Philosophical

Society, he worked to further efforts to excavate such items. In addition, Jefferson had a great interest in the lives and customs of Native Americans.

Upon receiving a question about Native American life in the state of Virginia, he wrote a description of how he was part of an excavation of a burial ground that had previously been titled, "The Indian Graves". It was there he found multiple human remains, and he learned more about burial cultures and customs. This burial ground was located in the vicinity of Monticello.

4) Jefferson was obsessed with good food.

Again, due to his time in France, Jefferson fell in love with fine French cuisine, and he was determined to always have good food at his table. One of the slaves he took with him to France, named James Hemings, was told that he should learn how to cook French cuisine so that he could do so upon their return to the States. Jefferson also added that if Hemings did so, he would give him his freedom.

5) Jefferson was a passionate farmer.

Jefferson owned quite a bit of land with Monticello, and he was very passionate about the land, especially in relation to the young country. Even though he'd grown up wealthy, he cared about the lower-class citizens of the US who had to work the land to make a living. He wanted the US to be a success with its agriculture. Part of the reason for that was so that the states didn't need to rely so heavily on other countries for assistance.

Because of his passion and his study, Jefferson was one of the very first farmers in the country to use crop rotation on his own land. He even worked to better the design of the plow to create more efficiency.

6) Jefferson was basically an architect.

Thomas Jefferson gives new meaning to the phrase, "jack of all trades", because he dabbled in almost every area of knowledge it is possible to study. He was an architect, and he loved designing buildings. His magnificent home at Monticello is a testament to that. But his designs didn't end there. He was the designer of the rotunda at the University of Virginia and the Virginia State Capitol in the city of Richmond. He called architecture the "hobby of my old age", showcasing his humility once again. Both his home Monticello and the University of Virginia are on the World Heritage List.

7) Jefferson was a stargazer.

And so, Jefferson's passions continued. He loved astronomy. Since he was the founder of the University of Virginia, he was able to design the curriculum. He made sure that astronomy was part of it, and he might have even designed the very first observatory in America.

8) Jefferson might have had a bad relationship with his parents.

Even though Jefferson was greatly influenced by his father's work ethic, Peter Jefferson died when Jefferson was only 14 years of age. We already know that Jefferson was an extensive letter-writer and yet, nothing exists of correspondence between himself and his father, nor even he and his mother. Some scholars believe that this could hint at some sort of distance between himself and his parents. However, there was a fire at his father's farm in 1770, so any remaining letters could have been burned at that time. But according to Jefferson's letters between him and his siblings, there was love and respect and a good relationship between them.

9) Jefferson was accused of an affair with a slave during his presidential election.

Sally Hemings was a very young woman when she accompanied Jefferson's second daughter Mary, to Paris. Jefferson remained there for five years, until 1789, and some scholars believe that this was the time in which he and Sally Hemings, a slave, began a relationship. There are no details about that relationship and what it fully entailed and whether or not it was a kind one. During the time of Jefferson's return from France and even during his presidency, Sally gave birth to six children, but only four of them ever reached adulthood.

Many historians believe that these were Jefferson's children, and he was accused of using his slave as a mistress by a journalist named James Callendar while he was trying to run for his first term as president. These rumors circulated throughout the Virginia newspapers at the time, and even though these were not modern times, and these kinds of relationships were quite normal, no one wanted to air their "dirty laundry" about such things. Jefferson replied to none of these rumors or attempted to defend himself in any way.

But surprisingly, nothing seemed to happen, even though Callendar tried his best to discredit Jefferson to keep him from running. Jefferson easily won his reelection, and there was no longer any shade on his reputation because of Sally. Nothing is recorded about her children that were any different from other slaves on the plantation. In later years, family members of Jefferson's were questioned about this affair, and there was some confusion as to who the father could have been. Some family members suggested that it was one of Jefferson's nephews, either Peter or Samuel Carr. But there wasn't certainty on that fact.

Jefferson's fatherhood of at least some of these children seemed even more likely when two of Hemings' children were allowed to leave Monticello without problem in 1822. And two others were given their freedom after Jefferson's death. Jefferson didn't free any others, so that hints towards some sort of connection he had to her children.

10) Abigail Adams was Jefferson's closest female friend.

Thomas Jefferson and Abigail Adams met in 1784, and she wrote to her sister about him after their first meeting. At the time, both the Adams and Jefferson family were living in Paris, and that was how they'd met. Abigail was feeling a little out of place, and Jefferson was still working through his grief at the loss of his wife. He had known John Adams for many years at that point because of their political work during the revolution, but it was only once in Paris that he got to know Adams' wife.

He visited their home often, and together, like strangers in an unknown land, they bonded and enjoyed a very close friendship. There were nine months they had in Paris together, and their families became very close as well. Jefferson and Abigail enjoyed many of the same interests, and so their relationship blossomed. After those nine months were over, the Adams' moved to London where John Adams had different work to do. Jefferson was heartbroken at the loss of them, and it must have felt like another grief.

They continued their correspondence, but then things began to change. Jefferson and Adams both returned to the states, and Adams became president with Jefferson serving as vice-president. Their differences in political opinion had become all too apparent, and as Adams was leaving office to make way for Jefferson to take his place, he tried his best to undermine him by working hard to add more Federalist judges.

This broke their relationship, and there was no contact between John and Abigail Adams and Thomas Jefferson in more than twelve years. But in 1804, after Jefferson lost his daughter Mary, Abigail did write to him again, and they resumed a bit of correspondence in which they hashed out their differences and what had gone down between John Adams and Jefferson in the previous years.

But at the time, John Adams knew nothing of this correspondence, and it was very unusual for a woman and man to speak to one another in letters. They were honest and forthright, and even though Jefferson offered friendship to Abigail, she refused him because of her loyalty to her husband who had been hurt by the past issues between them.

In the end, John Adams eventually wrote to him in 1812, and Adams and Jefferson continued with their friendship until the end of their lives. Perhaps Abigail had said something to him and encouraged her husband to heal what had been lost? We'll never know.

11) Jefferson was a prolific writer.

Writing, not speaking was Jefferson's superpower, and it sure showed throughout his life's work, whether it was his time as a lawyer or his time as president. Even after he retired to Monticello, his life was consumed by writing in more ways than one. We of course know about his famous writing of the Declaration of Independence, but he also had tons of letters written between himself and very famous historical figures. Together, the documents of Thomas Jefferson's that were given to the Library of Congress numbered about 27,000. Now, that's a real writer. He even wrote over 19,000 letters throughout the course of his life.

12) Jefferson went on a hunger strike!

If you can believe it, Jefferson asked for a day of fasting as well as prayer after the British government closed the Boston harbor. This occurred as a response to the fiery Boston Tea Party which occurred as a result of the Tea Tax. He was still a member of the Virginia House of Burgesses at this point, and he encouraged others to join him in this day of prayer and fasting. It was a success, and this helped to fuel the fire for the revolution as well as anti-British sentiments.

13) Jefferson's face is immortalized and not just on Mount Rushmore.

Ok, we all know that Jefferson's face is on Mount Rushmore along with Washington, Roosevelt, and Lincoln. He's also of course shown on the Jefferson Memorial in the Tidal Basin in D.C. which has a 19-foot statue of him. This was dedicated in 1943 which was the 200th anniversary of his birth. Not only that, but his face is also on the elusive and rare $2 bill as well as the nickel!

14) Jefferson was also a linguist.

It's not incredibly surprising, what with all his other accomplishments, that our third president spoke other languages besides English. Besides English, Jefferson was able to speak French, Italian, Spanish, Latin, and Greek. These skills would have helped him in his interactions while working as the US Minister to France as well as his ability to study ancient texts written in Latin and Greek. Italian might have helped him in his pursuit of the finer things in life such as opera, and Spanish might have been of use to him as he dealt with North American land changing hands between the Spanish and the French.

Each president had their own unique stories that hid behind their time as president as well as filled the rest of their days. In Jefferson's case, he was only president for eight years, and so he had the rest of his life to fill with interesting and special hobbies, skills, and achievements. Not all of his stories are happy ones, and there were certainly some dark moments, but one thing we could say for him is that he had a very full and fascinating life. He truly is the embodiment of what we call a Renaissance man.

Final Words

Most times, a hero's great story is humbled by the fact that he had humble beginnings and he worked himself up from there. That is the American Dream, right? But Thomas Jefferson didn't quite have humble beginnings. His family were wealthy landowners, and especially through his mother, they were of a high social status. Jefferson had everything to support him as he entered into the world. He lived on a large farm that his father owned and worked. His family owned slaves until he became the land and slave owner upon his father's death.

He was given the best tutors and the best education. He came out on the other side, full of knowledge and promise, ready to enter the world prepared to contribute what he had to offer. That is the thing, isn't it? Even though Jefferson didn't have to fight to gain the money and education that he had, he still had the initiative and the drive to give back to the world. He used his skills and his gifts to do what he could for those who needed it.

For example, he wanted to fight against the old systems when they were still under British rule. He used his skill as a lawyer to help those smaller landowners who needed help. He kept them working and retaining the land that they owned. He used his skill as a writer to help draft some of the most famous political documents in the world, giving us beautiful, eloquent phrases such as "all men are created equal." His fight with the pen helped pave the way to breaking free from British control and tyranny.

After he became president, he worked towards helping the young country grow and develop into an independent one. Likely his greatest contribution to the presidency was the timely purchase of the Louisiana territory, giving the country the strength and backbone it needed to become one of the most powerful countries in the world. He aided the economy, making it stronger. He assisted with international relations.

After the presidency, even though his time in the public eye was over, he wasn't yet finished giving things to the world, adding to his legacy. He continued to improve his mind, if nothing else, then for the sake of his own pleasure. But with his knowledge, he designed and founded the University of Virginia, which is one of the foremost institutions in the US. He patched up old relationships, writing with fondness to his old friend and comrade in arms against tyranny, John Adams.

He had a loving family who spent time with him, learning from him, and enjoying his company. And then he came full circle it seemed, dying on the 4th of July, the very day his famous document was approved to be sent to England. Thomas Jefferson, despite his many earthly belongings, died in debt and amongst problems. He didn't do everything right in his life, and many of his viewpoints were problematic and wrong, contradicting the views he wrote about and fought for so doggedly.

However, he gave what he had to the world. He gave his intelligence, his time, his abilities, his acquired skills, and even when he was sick and on his deathbed, he continued to give. He didn't want to be done working, learning, developing, growing. Thomas Jefferson did so much more than serve as the third president of the United States. He was someone who took what privileges he'd been given, and he used them to the advantage of many others.

Where would the country be if Thomas Jefferson had never existed? Or if he had existed but not chosen to share his wonderful gifts with us? It's likely that without him, the Revolution might not have turned out as it had, or perhaps, it might not have even begun on such strong footing. Thomas Jefferson is remembered for this: his vigilance in caring for the nation that he helped to bring about, but also because he loved the idea of gaining knowledge and sharing it with the world. Even his own tombstone, written by him, focuses more on the ideas he spread and shared, rather than the titles he held. It doesn't even mention his time as president.

Perhaps he wasn't even proud of the foremost title of power one can hold in the US, but he was proud that he had been the one to pen the famous words which made up the Declaration of Independence. With his words, a nation sparked to life, fueling a fire for freedom in the hearts and minds of many. It's safe to say that Thomas Jefferson left a legacy with which not many people can compete.

Timeline Of Thomas Jefferson

❖ **April 13, 1743**

➢ Thomas Jefferson is born to Jane Randolph Jefferson and Peter Jefferson on Shadwell Plantation in Albemarle County, Virginia.

❖ **1746**

➢ Jefferson's first memory is of taking a fifty-mile horseback with his father's slave through the wilds of Virginia.

❖ **1752**

➢ Jefferson begins his education at age nine, and he is given private tutoring under a minister. He spends nine months out of the year with his teacher.

❖ **1757**

➢ Jefferson's father, Peter, passes away, and Jefferson is only 14. He is left with a lot of land.

❖ **1760**

➢ Jefferson attends the college of William and Mary.

❖ **1762**

> Thomas begins to study law with the famous George Wythe.

❖ **1767**

> Becomes an official, barred, Virginia lawyer and is allowed to practice law in front of a general court. He focuses mainly on land disputes.

❖ **1769-1774**

> He is a member of the Virginia House of Burgesses.

❖ **January 1, 1772**

> Jefferson marries Martha Wayles Skelton at her family's plantation.

> September 27: Martha, their first child is born, the one who would live to adulthood and be the final Jefferson child alive at his death in 1826.

❖ **1773**

> Sally Hemings, a slave woman, is born on the Wayles plantation. She is most likely the child of the now Mrs. Jefferson's father, making them half-sisters.

- ❖ **1774**
  - ➤ Jefferson writes "A Summary View of the Right of British America" which helped to build his popularity as a skilled and eloquent writer who knew exactly what the fight was all about.
  - ➤ Retires from his time as a lawyer, selling his practice.

- ❖ **1775**
  - ➤ Elected to Second Continental Congress.

- ❖ **1776**
  - ➤ Jefferson is put into a group to draft the Declaration of Independence, but because of his skills, Jefferson wrote the whole thing by himself. Later, the other members would give their ideas for adjustments or changes.
  - ➤ Is elected to the Virginia House of Delegates and served until 1779.
  - ➤ His mother, Jane Randolph, passes away.

- ❖ **1777**
  - ➤ Writes and drafts the "Virginia Statute for Religious Freedoms" or "Virginia Bill for Establishing Religious Freedoms. This portrayed

Jefferson's beliefs that God existed but he had no real part in the life of humans and had no place in politics.

❖ **1778**

➤ Mary Jefferson is born, and she is the other child who lived to adulthood but later died in childbirth.

❖ **1779**

➤ Serves as Governor of Virginia until 1781.

❖ **1780**

➤ Elected to be part of the American Philosophical Society in 1780.

❖ **1781**

➤ British troops at Monticello force Jefferson to run away.

➤ He returns home to Monticello after resigning from the office of governor.

❖ **November 6, 1782**

➤ His wife Martha dies from complications in childbirth, and Jefferson is heartbroken.

❖ **1783**

➢ Elected as delegate to the Confederation Congress.

❖ **1784**

➢ Begins his service in France as Minister of the United States. He holds this position until 1789. His daughters and the slave Sally Hemings eventually join him in Paris.

➢ Meets Abigail Adams, and they begin a friendship as well as a long correspondence.

❖ **1785**

➢ *Notes on the State of Virginia*, his only book, is published. He worked on it during his stay at Monticello.

❖ **February 23, 1790**

➢ Martha Jefferson marries Thomas Mann Randolph.

❖ **1790-1793**

➢ Serves as the Secretary of State of the new US under George Washington's presidency.

- ❖ **1795**
  - ➤ Jefferson and Sally Hemings allegedly have their first daughter together, named Harriet. She dies two years later.

- ❖ **October 13, 1797**
  - ➤ Jefferson's other living daughter, Mary, marries John Wayles Epps.

- ❖ **1796**
  - ➤ Jefferson begins to run for presidency, but he is beaten by his friend John Adams. Political parties are starting to form, and Jefferson is head of the Republicans or Democratic-Republicans.

- ❖ **1797- 1801**
  - ➤ Serves as vice-president under John Adams, even though they didn't get along anymore because of their very different political views. John Adams is a Federalist and Jefferson a Republican.
  - ➤ During this time, he writes "A Manual for Parliamentary Practice" which was used for many years in Congressional meetings.

- ❖ **1801-09**
  - ➤ Thomas Jefferson becomes the third president of the United States after beating his friend John Adams.
  - ➤ John Adams tried to undermine his friend's presidency through the "midnight judges".
  - ➤ Louisiana Purchase takes place in 1803, doubling the size of the US.
  - ➤ He launches the Lewis and Clark expedition to go and explore the new land and bring back useful information.

- ❖ **April 17, 1804**
  - ➤ Jefferson's daughter, Mary, dies in childbirth, leaving Martha the only child of Jefferson left.
  - ➤ Once hearing about this, Abigail Adams resumes her correspondence with Jefferson after a break because of his issues with John Adams.

- ❖ **1807**
  - ➤ Jefferson creates the Embargo Act of 1807, which bans shipping with Europe. It was a failure, and he lost a lot of popularity after that.

- ❖ **1809**

  - ➢ Leaves office after two terms as president.

  - ➢ His first term was more successful than his second.

  - ➢ He returns to Monticello to live out the rest of his days.

- ❖ **1812**

  - ➢ Resumes friendship and correspondence with old friend, John Adams. They "bury the hatchet" and wrote of their fondness for one another in the end.

- ❖ **1815**

  - ➢ Retires from his role as president of the American Philosophical Society after many years.

- ❖ **1819**

  - ➢ Jefferson founds the University of Virginia.

- ❖ **March 7, 1825**

  - ➢ University of Virginia is open for enrollment.

- ❖ **1826**

  - ➢ After many health complications, Thomas Jefferson dies in his home at Monticello on July 4th, and John Adams dies on the same day, a few hours later.

Bibliography

"5 Surprising Facts about Thomas Jefferson." N.d. Mr. Jefferson Monticello. Accessed October 8, 2021. https://www.monticello.org/site/blog-and-community/5-surprising-facts-about-thomas-jefferson.

"Biography of Thomas Jefferson." 2012. Let.rug.nl. Accessed September 29, 2021. http://www.let.rug.nl/usa/biographies/thomas-jefferson/prelude-to-the-presidency.php.

"Famous Jefferson Quotes". 2019. Mr. Jefferson Monticello. Accessed October 8, 2021. https://www.monticello.org/site/research-and-collections/famous-jefferson-quotes.

"Fun Facts about Thomas Jefferson." 2016. Boston Tea Partyship. Accessed October 12, 2021. https://www.bostonteapartyship.com/thomas-jefferson-facts.

"The Letters of Thomas Jefferson 1743-1826." n.d. Www.let.rug.nl. Accessed October 6, 2021. http://www.let.rug.nl/usa/presidents/thomas-jefferson/letters-of-thomas-jefferson/.

Biography.com Editors. 2014. "Thomas Jefferson Biography". https://www.biography.com/us-president/thomas-jefferson.

Francavilla, Lisa. 2021. "Jefferson, Thomas and His Family." Encyclopedia Virginia. Accessed October 10, 2021. https://encyclopediavirginia.org/entries/jefferson-thomas-and-his-family/.

Freidel, Frank, Hugh Sidey, and White. 2006. *The Presidents of the United States of America*. Washington, D.C.: White House Historical Association

Gelles, Edith B. 2018. "Abigail and Tom." Omohundro Institute of Early American History & Culture. Accessed October 8, 2021. https://blog.oieahc.wm.edu/abigail-and-tom/#:~:text=Those%20nine%20months%20together%20were,for%20the%20 Adams%2DJefferson%20 friendship.

History.com Editors. 2009. "Treaty of Paris Signed." HISTORY. https://www.history.com/this-day-in-history/treaty-of-paris-signed.

Konig, David. "Jefferson, Thomas and the Practice of Law – Encyclopedia Virginia." n.d. Accessed September 29, 2021. https://encyclopediavirginia.org/entries/jefferson-thomas-and-the-practice-of-law/.

Martin, Russell L. 1990. "Jefferson's Cause of Death." Mr. Jefferson Monticello. Accessed October 6, 2021. https://www.monticello.org/site/research-and-collections/jeffersons-cause-death.

NCC Staff. 2021. "10 Facts about Thomas Jefferson for His Birthday." National Constitution Center. Accessed October 7, 2021. https://constitutioncenter.org/blog/10-facts-about-thomas-jefferson-for-his-birthday.

Onuf, Peter. n.d. "Thomas Jefferson: Campaigns and Elections." Miller Center. Accessed October 6, 2021. https://millercenter.org/president/jefferson/campaigns-and-elections

Onuf, Peter. n.d. "Thomas Jefferson: Family Life." Miller Center. Accessed October 6, 2021. https://millercenter.org/president/jefferson/family-life

Onuf, Peter. n.d. "Thomas Jefferson: Foreign Affairs." Miller Center. Accessed October 6, 2021. https://millercenter.org/president/jefferson/foreign-affairs.

Onuf, Peter. n.d. "Thomas Jefferson: Life After the Presidency." Miller Center. Accessed October 6, 2021. https://millercenter.org/president/jefferson/familylifehttps://millercenter.org/president/jefferson/life-after-the-presidency

Onuf, Peter. n.d. "Thomas Jefferson: Life Before the Presidency." Miller Center. Accessed September 29, 2021. https://millercenter.org/president/jefferson/life-before-the-presidency.

Wilson, Gaye. 1997. "American Philosophical Society." Mr. Jefferson Monticello. Accessed October 10, 2021. https://www.monticello.org/site/research-and-collections/american-philosophical-society.

Zechmeister, Gene. 2010. "Jefferson's Excavation of an Indian Burial Mound." Mr. Jefferson Monticello. Accessed October 6, 2021. https://www.monticello.org/site/research-and-collections/jeffersons-excavation-indian-burial-mound.

www.ingramcontent.com/pod-product-compliance
Lightning Source LLC
Chambersburg PA
CBHW070930120626
46546CB00004B/1377

* 9 7 8 1 9 5 9 0 1 8 9 9 5 *